W9-AGZ-664

GAYLORD

YouTube

ABDO
Publishing Company

TECHNOLOGY
PIONEERS

YouTube

THE COMPANY AND ITS FOUNDERS

by Rebecca Rowell

Content Consultant
Patricia G. Lange, PhD
Department of Anthropology
University of Southern California

CREDITS

Published by ABDO Publishing Company, 8000 West 78th Street, Edina, Minnesota 55439. Copyright © 2011 by Abdo Consulting Group, Inc. International copyrights reserved in all countries. No part of this book may be reproduced in any form without written permission from the publisher. The Essential Library™ is a trademark and logo of ABDO Publishing Company.

Printed in the United States of America,
North Mankato, Minnesota
112010
012011

Editor: Amy Van Zee
Copy Editor: Sarah Beckman
Interior Design and Production: Craig Hinton
Cover Design: Emily Love

Library of Congress Cataloging-in-Publication Data
Rowell, Rebecca, 1968- author.
 YouTube : the company and its founders / By Rebecca Rowell.
     p. cm. -- (Technology pioneers)
 Includes bibliographical references and index.
 ISBN 978-1-61714-813-2
 1. YouTube (Firm)--History. 2. YouTube (Electronic resource) I.
Title.
 TK5105.8868.Y68R69 2011
 006.7--dc22
                                        2010043379

TABLE OF CONTENTS

Chapter 1	The Wedding Viewed Worldwide	6
Chapter 2	Steven Chen	16
Chapter 3	Chad Hurley	24
Chapter 4	Jawed Karim	32
Chapter 5	Meeting at PayPal	40
Chapter 6	"Broadcast Yourself"	46
Chapter 7	Social Impact	56
Chapter 8	Sold!	66
Chapter 9	New Owner, Same YouTube	78
Chapter 10	Politics, Pop Music, and Beyond	88
Timeline		96
Essential Facts		100
Glossary		102
Additional Resources		104
Source Notes		106
Index		110
About the Author		112

YouTube has changed the way people share and view videos on the Internet.

THE
WEDDING VIEWED
WORLDWIDE

F amily and friends gathered at a church in St. Paul, Minnesota, on June 20, 2009, to witness and celebrate the marriage of Jill Peterson and Kevin Heinz. But this was not just any wedding—the guests were about to experience something unusual.

Rather than choose a traditional song for the processional, such as "Here Comes the Bride" or Pachelbel's "Canon in D Major," Heinz and Peterson chose a pop song. Chris Brown's "Forever" began to play. And when the music started, the bridal party danced. The ushers, the groomsmen, and the bridesmaids all boogied their way down the aisle. After heading toward the altar in solo and pair dances, the ushers, groomsmen, and bridesmaids returned to the back of the church and started over, performing as a group. Swaying onward, the group parted. Suddenly, the groom appeared by way of somersault. After they all reached the altar, he walked back down the aisle to greet his bride, who was shimmying her way toward him.

When the bride and groom reached their destination, the music quieted. The procession had ended, but the church was not silent. The guests clapped and cheered, including the officiant. They had just witnessed a joyous and unconventional wedding procession. And in a matter of days, thousands more would view the celebration.

GOING VIRAL

As many couples do, Heinz and Peterson had a videographer record their wedding ceremony. Doing

STILL POPULAR

In mid-December 2009, the number of views of Heinz and Peterson's video was more than 33 million. In October 2010, the number of views exceeded 50 million. The newlyweds wanted to use the popularity gained by their video for a good cause. They created a Web site where visitors can donate money to combat domestic violence.

so would preserve the event and allow the newlyweds to enjoy the memories of their special day for years to come. The couple could also share the video with friends and family members. On July 19, Heinz and Johnson put their video, titled "JK Wedding Entrance Dance," online and let family and friends know where to find it. The couple had uploaded it to YouTube, a site designed specifically for sharing videos.

Launched in 2005 by three young men in California, YouTube had become a popular site. Founders Steve Chen, Chad Hurley, and Jawed Karim had developed YouTube as a means to share videos quickly and easily, and they encouraged users to broadcast themselves. The site arrived at a time when other social networking Web sites were emerging and gaining popularity. YouTube seemed to tap into humans' desire to be known by and connect with one another. The site caught on quickly and had been growing exponentially when Heinz and

Peterson uploaded their wedding video. People worldwide were uploading and viewing videos every day by the millions. Some videos were of television shows. Many were personal videos made by the users, including footage of babies taking their first steps, aspiring singers and comics performing, and craftspeople teaching an art form. Family, friends, coworkers, and complete strangers near and far eagerly watched, connecting with users across town and around the world through shared interests and experiences—and users were making the site a hit.

Soon after Heinz and Peterson uploaded their wedding video on July 19, view numbers

WHAT MAKES A VIDEO GO VIRAL?

Going viral can do great things for video creators. In the case of Heinz and Peterson, the newlyweds appeared live on national television. For others, going viral can have a greater impact, such as resulting in financial gains. For example, the popularity of a pop star's music video could lead to an increase in sales of that star's latest CD or online music. The increase in views of a commercial promoting a company's product could also result in an increase in sales of that product.

Jake Nyberg of the video production and marketing firm Three Volts has received calls from clients who demand they go viral. But what exactly makes a video go viral is not certain. As Nyberg explains, "It's an interesting question because if there were a magic formula, there'd be a lot more people doing it."[1] Humor and genuineness of emotion and the human experience seem most appealing to viewers. As for trying to create a viral video, Nyberg explained, "I often tell people who want to go viral: viral is not a strategy, it's an outcome. Can you make a good attempt? Certainly."[2]

started increasing. The video spread in the Twin Cities of Minneapolis and St. Paul through local print and television news. But the video was also spread through Twitter and Facebook, which are popular forms of social networking media. Within days, thousands of strangers—many more people than had attended their celebration—had witnessed the couple's wedding ceremony. It had gone viral, spreading like a virus as more and more people learned about the video, accessed the Web site, and viewed the clip. The video had done exactly what YouTube's founders had hoped.

By July 24, the video had been viewed almost 2 million times. Actor Ashton Kutcher learned of the video and sent its YouTube link to his 2 million Twitter followers. From there, it became the subject of blogs. Eventually, the video caught the attention of national news outlets.

Eager to capitalize on the video's popularity, NBC's *Today Show* asked Heinz and Peterson to appear. On July 25, the couple and their wedding party performed the now-famous wedding dance live on national television. This only added to the video's popularity. The following day, the video had been viewed more than 6 million times.

Huang Yixin, *left,* and Wei Wei are former college roommates who became popular for their humorous lip-synching videos on YouTube.

THE POWER OF YOUTUBE

Most YouTube videos do not receive the amount of attention gained by "JK Wedding Entrance Dance," but there are videos that go viral—increasingly so as social networks continue to grow in popularity. Sometimes, these videos are of celebrities, such as the pop singer Lady Gaga, whose music videos garner views in the millions. Other times, they are made by people such as Heinz and Peterson, whose video showcased a special day in their lives.

Jake Nyberg, a partner of the video production and marketing firm Three Volts, explained that part of the wedding video's appeal is its universal theme—weddings take place worldwide, and people can relate to and appreciate their meaning. People tend to like love stories and happy endings. He also noted its authenticity, saying, "It's human. It's novel. You say, oh man, I've never seen anything like that before."[3]

Technology has made the world seem smaller than ever. Webcams and blogs allow people to connect far more easily than was possible a generation ago. YouTube has added another means for sharing by providing a venue for users with even the most minimal computer skills to upload and watch videos quickly and easily.

By posting their videos on YouTube, unknowns around the globe make themselves available to the world—to teach, to share experiences, to show off their talents, and to make others smile or laugh, as Heinz and Peterson did.

"Such is its impact that it has become difficult to remember a time before YouTube, particularly for those millions of teens that have grown up with the internet over the last five years."[4]

—Adam Hartley, "YouTube is five years old this week"

The couple's success is a story shared by many others who have posted videos on YouTube—unknowns and celebrities alike. But access to fame is only one aspect of the YouTube phenomenon. The site has also become a valuable resource for sharing information about current events, such as footage from disaster-stricken areas or a political candidate's campaign messages. YouTube is also an archive that allows users to easily find and view decades-old television programs and performances by entertainers that might otherwise be inaccessible.

YouTube has paved the way for all kinds of computer users—from average individuals to pop stars to entertainment businesses—to connect with one another. But with all its success, the landmark Web site has not been without challenges. YouTube has contended with many issues, including copyright violation and concerns about the appropriateness of some content. Many videos must be removed for these reasons. In some countries, such as Pakistan, the site is blocked entirely, threatening YouTube's global success.

But YouTube has allowed users to reach people they could not without the site. All this is possible because of the work of Steve Chen, Chad Hurley, and Jawed Karim. Their launch of this video-

YOUTUBE AND MEMES

A meme is a concept, fad, or phenomenon that spreads quickly within a culture, often through imitation. The Internet has helped memes spread because it allows people to connect all over the world. Links to videos and images can be shared through e-mail, Facebook, blogs, Twitter, and other means. Oftentimes, memes feed off each other, and YouTube has contributed to this as videos go viral. For example, "JK Wedding Entrance Dance" has been re-created on television by news anchors, on *Dancing with the Stars—Australia*, and on *The Office*. Other brides and grooms mimicked the dancing and recorded their performances. A spin-off video named "Unexpected Divorce Intro" includes actors depicting the couple divorcing in court, complete with court officers dancing, including a judge jiving to Chris Brown's "Forever." Videos of all these performances can be found on YouTube.

sharing Web site in 2005 quickly changed the lives of computer users worldwide—including two young newlyweds from Minnesota—and continues to affect the lives of millions of computer users every day. +

Ashton Kutcher helped popularize the "JK Wedding Entrance Dance" video by posting the link on Twitter.

Steve Chen in 2007

STEVEN CHEN

S teven Shih Chen is one of YouTube's three
founders. Born in Taipei, Taiwan, in 1978, he
usually goes by the nickname Steve. Steve's
father owned a successful trading company in Taipei.
The business was doing so well that Mr. Chen

decided to expand to the United States. He chose Chicago, Illinois, as the location for his new US branch and moved his family to Prospect Heights, a suburb of the bustling Midwestern city. At the time, Steve was eight years old.

LIVING IN TWO CULTURES

Moving to a new city and starting a new school is challenging for any youngster. It was particularly challenging for Steve, who did not speak English. The Chens—Steve's parents and younger brother, Ricky—spoke Mandarin, a form of Chinese. When Steve began attending a US school in the third grade, he was not placed in a special program to learn English. He was simply assigned to a class and picked up the language from being exposed to it. But children tend to acquire language quickly, and young Steve soon learned to

CHINA

After moving to the United States and learning to speak English, Steve continued to speak Chinese, his native language, at home. Chinese is the primary language of Asia and has many variations: Mandarin, Wu, Min, Gan, Hakka, Xiang, and Cantonese. These languages differ mostly in pronunciation and vocabulary. Worldwide, more people speak Chinese as their native tongue than any other language.

China, a Communist country, has made headlines for blocking access to YouTube. In March 2008, the site was blocked after riots that took place in Tibet. The site was blocked again in 2009. China has blocked Web sites and television broadcasts that report on political topics.

Steve lived in Taipei, Taiwan, until he was eight.

speak the language of his new homeland. In a way, Steve lived two lives. Thanks to his childhood in Taiwan, in his home, Steve was Taiwanese. He shared his native language, cuisine, and cultural heritage with his family. Away from home, he was a typical American boy. Though he was often the only Asian student at school, Steve explained as an adult that he and his brother did not feel any different from other Midwestern kids.

EDUCATION

When Steve was 13 years old, he moved to Illinois Mathematics and Science Academy (IMSA), a boarding school in Aurora, Illinois, approximately 45 miles (72 km) from his home. IMSA set aside Wednesdays for exploration. Rather than attend their usual classes, students were free to investigate personal areas of interest.

IMSA was an ideal school for Steve, who had an interest in and gift for technology. He focused on computer science. Steve was a smart and dedicated student, as were many of his classmates. Some of them studied

TAIPEI, TAIWAN

Steve lived in Taipei until he was eight but remembers little of the city. However, he has become acquainted with his birthplace through visits. Located at the northern tip of Taiwan, Taipei is the island nation's largest city, with an area of 105 square miles (272 sq km) and more than 2.6 million residents. Taipei is Taiwan's cultural, economic, and political center.

Taiwan and mainland China are separated by the Taiwan Strait. Chinese immigrants founded Taipei in the early 1700s. The location became a valuable trade center. Taiwan was declared a Chinese province in 1886, and Taipei became the provincial capital.

Taipei grew dramatically after World War II (1939–1945) and reached a population of 1 million in the early 1960s. By the mid-1970s, another million people inhabited Taipei. By the mid-1990s, it was one of the most densely populated areas in the world.

Taipei is a modern city with many high-rise buildings, including Taipei 101, an office building that was the world's tallest building from 2003 to 2007. Taipei boasts considerable green space, which is promoted by the subtropical climate.

ILLINOIS MATHEMATICS AND SCIENCE ACADEMY

Illinois Mathematics and Science Academy (IMSA) had been operating only a few years when Steve became a student there. Founded in 1985, IMSA is a college preparatory school that enrolls 650 students in grades 10, 11, and 12. Programs focus on advanced studies in engineering, mathematics, science, and technology. Tuition is free, and students are required to live at the school. IMSA was one of the first schools to provide Internet access to its students.

advanced mathematics such as calculus at age 13. Steve said about his experience at IMSA, "It was also the time I learned that I wasn't the smartest kid anymore."[1]

Following his graduation from IMSA, Steve decided to stay in his home state for college. He chose the University of Illinois at Urbana-Champaign because of its computer science program, which is one of the best in the nation. In addition, IMSA has a strong connection with the university, which likely ensured approval of his application. The University of Illinois at Urbana-Champaign was the only college Steve applied to, and he was accepted. Steve continued to pursue his interest in computers by majoring in computer science.

Many of his classmates at IMSA also enrolled at the university, so Steve started his freshman year with familiar faces and friends. And he spent time with college classmates outside of class doing what he loved: writing code. Using special language understood by computers, Steve developed instructions to make computers do specific tasks. Steve enjoyed college, especially the resources it made available to him and other students. However, he did not complete his college studies.

A DIFFERENT PATH

Rather than finish his bachelor's degree, Chen took a different path. With more than half of his course work completed, the young man moved to the West Coast. In 1998, an opportunity arose that he could not ignore.

A new company named Confinity had formed in California. Confinity was a technology company focused on the growing online retail industry. The company created PayPal to help people securely buy and sell online. Confinity was cofounded by Max Levchin, a former student at both the University of Illinois at Urbana-Champaign and IMSA. According to Levchin, the two schools are a great combination, creating "hard-core smart, hardworking, nonspoiled" foundling engineers ideal for start-up companies

UNIVERSITY OF ILLINOIS AT URBANA-CHAMPAIGN

The University of Illinois at Urbana-Champaign was founded in 1867. It has two supercomputer centers, which are extremely powerful research tools for performing calculations, simulations, and processing data. The Department of Computer Science was created in 1964, though faculty had been working on computers since the 1940s. The program has several successful alumni. Steve Dorner developed the e-mail program Eudora in 1988. Marc Andreessen and Eric Bina developed most of Mosaic, which launched in 1993 and led to the Internet boom. In 1998, Max Levchin founded PayPal.

such as Confinity. Chen was a product of those schools. "The kind of people that IMSA attracts are the kind of people very prone to choose their own path," explained Levchin.[2]

By accepting Levchin's job offer, Chen did choose his own path. Not surprisingly, Chen's family was concerned about his decision. His brother, Ricky, said, "We told him it was risky; he just had a few months left [to complete his college degree]. But he was determined to give it a shot."[3] +

The University of Illinois at Urbana-Champaign

Chad Hurley in 2010

CHAD HURLEY

Chad Meredith Hurley was born in Birdsboro, Pennsylvania, in 1977. He is the middle child of Donald and JoAnn Hurley. His father was a financial consultant, and his mother was a teacher. From a young age, Chad's talents and interest in art were evident. He particularly enjoyed painting and sculpting and spent a lot of time doing both.

Chad was proud of his artistic creations and tried selling some of his artwork from his front lawn, just as many children try to sell lemonade. His confidence to do something many might consider different came from his father. Of his father, Chad has said, "[He] taught me the power of positive thinking and just going for it."[1]

EDUCATION

While a boy, Chad showed interest and talent in another area: computers. Like a lot of young people, he enjoyed playing computer games. And with his interest and ability in art, Chad was drawn to Web design and computer animation. Surfing the Internet allowed him a seemingly unlimited selection of Web sites to study and learn about good—and bad—design. For his formal studies, Chad attended Twin Valley High School. Chad's mother was a teacher at the high school he attended.

When he was not busy doing homework or running on the cross-country and track teams, Chad tinkered with electronics. When he was a freshman, Chad won the third-place prize in a national electronics competition. His entry was an amplifier, a device that increases power and is often used with stereo systems.

Chad graduated from high school in 1995 and became a college student in the fall of that year. At Indiana University of Pennsylvania, his childhood interests in computers and art dominated his studies. Initially, Chad majored in computer science. However, his love of artistic endeavors won out over technology. Chad's father, Donald, explained, "Computer science, that was too technical, too mechanical for Chad. He wanted to be on the creative side."[2] As a result, Chad decided

BIRDSBORO, PENNSYLVANIA

Chad Hurley and Steve Chen were born in dramatically different cities—not only in terms of culture and history, but also size and climate. Hurley's hometown, Birdsboro, is located in southeastern Pennsylvania. The city is named after William Bird, an iron maker who founded a forge in the area circa 1740. In 1771, Bird's son established Hopewell Furnace in the same area, and it became one of the largest producers of iron during the American Revolution (1775–1783). This was the beginning of industry coming to the area.

Birdsboro is quite small. In 1890, the town's population was 2,261. As of the 2000 census, the population of Birdsboro was 5,064. A well-known resident of Birdsboro was Daniel Boone, the pioneer and hunter made famous in books and films.

The area was once inhabited by the Delaware Indians, also known as the Lenape. It was later settled by immigrants from Germany and other European nations. The geography of the area is primarily mountainous, making hiking a popular activity. It provided Hurley with a good training ground for cross-country running.

Although Hurley no longer lives in Pennsylvania, he is still a fan of his home state. During a 2008 speech at his alma mater, Indiana University of Pennsylvania (IUP), Hurley said, "I'm proud to be from Pennsylvania, and I'm proud to be from IUP."[3]

to pursue a degree in fine arts, focusing on design and printmaking.

Chad continued to study Web sites to learn about and understand Web design and animation. He ran cross country for his college team and sold kitchen knives door-to-door, sometimes putting on product demonstrations in his friends' homes. During his demonstrations, he would cut through soda pop cans, just like the knives shown in some television commercials at that time. But this would not be his job for long.

THE NEXT STEP

Hurley completed his studies at Indiana University of Pennsylvania in 1999. Like so many soon-to-be college graduates, he started looking for work before he finished school. Hurley sent his résumé to prospective clients, including a new

STATE CROSS-COUNTRY CHAMPS

Chad was an athlete as well as an artist. Twin Valley High School won two state cross-country championships while he was a member of the team: in 1992 and 1994.

NEW AND OLD ARTISTIC MEDIUMS

Hurley's interest in Web design and computer animation relied on a new artistic medium. When he began exploring these genres, computers were relatively new—computers began being marketed to the public in the early 1980s. In contrast, printmaking has been built on a foundation of knowledge and experience that has developed over the past several hundred years. Originally a form of communication, printmaking techniques can be traced back to prehistoric times. Although today's printmakers have access to new forms of technology, some still use old methods. These include relief techniques such as woodcutting.

company named Confinity that specialized in online payments. He read about the company and its PayPal software in *Wired*, a technology magazine. Hurley received an immediate response. Just two days after inquiring about a position with the start-up company, Hurley flew to California for an interview.

The people at Confinity wanted to see Hurley's design skills, so they gave him an assignment: draw a logo for PayPal, the software that was the heart of the company's work. Hurley did not disappoint—the logo he designed as part of his job interview became PayPal's official logo. In less than a week, Hurley had read about Confinity, sent the company his résumé, flown across the country for an interview, and received a job offer. Hurley gladly accepted the offer and headed to the West Coast to start his new job as the

The design Hurley created in his job interview became PayPal's official logo. PayPal released this updated logo in August 2007.

company's first designer. He was the company's tenth employee.

While his job search had been ideal, Hurley did experience some difficulty. After moving to California, he struggled financially until he received his first paycheck. Hurley's limited funds prevented him from being able to rent an apartment right away. But he was not without a place to stay. While saving money to get his own place, Hurley slept on a friend's floor. This housing challenge was only

HONORING HIS COACH

Hurley's appreciation of and respect for his college track coach became evident in November 2008, when the school broke ground on a new building, the Kovalchick Convention and Athletic Complex. The 1999 graduate donated $1 million to name the Kovalchick complex's arena after his former coach, Ed Fry, who was retiring at the end of the school year. At the event, Hurley explained he was happy "to honor my old coach, Ed Fry, who has dedicated more than forty years to students and to IUP and is in his last year of coaching."[4]

temporary. Hurley's new position quickly provided him the money he needed to meet his housing needs and other living expenses. It also introduced him to coworkers who would become his friends and business partners: Steve Chen and Jawed Karim. +

Confinity developed the PayPal software to make shopping online safer.

YouTube cofounder Jawed Karim, *right*, was awarded the first Chancellor's No Boundaries award from the University of Illinois in 2007.

JAWED KARIM

J awed Karim was born in May 1979 in Merseberg, East Germany (present-day Germany). The following year, Jawed and his family moved to West Germany. Jawed spent much of his childhood in Europe, but he did not spend his entire youth there. The Karims moved to the United States in 1992. That year, Jawed's family settled in Maplewood, a suburb of St. Paul, Minnesota.

CURIOUS CHILD

Both of Jawed's parents were scientists. His father, Naimul, was a Bangladeshi chemist employed by 3M, a company headquartered in Minnesota. Christine, Jawed's mother, was a German professor of biochemistry at the University of Minnesota. Like his parents, Jawed was interested in science and technology. When he was young, Jawed often visited the laboratories where his parents worked. One day, one of his mother's coworkers explained to young Jawed how televisions and radios work. According to Christine, her son was completely taken with the information and told her about it during their drive home from the lab.

3M

Jawed's family moved to Minnesota when his father accepted a position with 3M. Minnesota Mining and Manufacturing, more commonly known as 3M, was founded in northern Minnesota in 1902. Throughout its more than 100 years in existence, the company has developed a variety of products. 3M developed the first waterproof sandpaper in the early 1920s. In 1925, a lab assistant developed masking tape. Subsequent inventions include cellophane tape (or Scotch Tape), Scotchgard Fabric Protector, and Post-it Notes.

During his childhood, Jawed spent a lot of time in the research labs at the University of Minnesota, where his mother was a biochemistry professor.

Naimul explained a bit of his son's upbringing and why the boy spent so much time at his parents' labs:

We didn't have anyone to take care of him, so we would bring him along to the lab. We would give him things to play with, like a magnetic stirring bar in a beaker of water. My wife usually took him to her work, and there were lots of physicists around. They commented to us that Jawed was almost like a sponge. At 10, 11 years old, he would just listen and observe everything.[1]

At this young age, Jawed showed interest in and talent with computers. When Jawed was ten years old, his father bought him a Commodore computer. It was a used computer, but that did not matter to Jawed. The boy spent a lot of time playing with the computer and quickly started writing code, a skill he would soon use to help others.

"It's very simple: I basically create things that I need myself. It just so happens that sometimes other people want to use that."[2]

—*Jawed Karim,
YouTube cofounder*

EDUCATION

Jawed attended St. Paul Central High School. While a student there, he put his interest in computers to good use. When he was 16, Jawed heard some teachers expressing frustration because the school did not have an e-mail system for them to use. The teenager promptly created an e-mail system for them. He did it for fun and to be helpful, not for pay.

During his senior year, Jawed tackled another computer task. This time, though, he was paid for his work. Jawed made eight dollars an hour creating a Web site for his mother's research lab at the University of Minnesota.

When Jawed graduated from high school in 1997, he planned to attend the University of Illinois at Urbana-Champaign. Naturally, he was going to major in computer science. However, the school did not accept him into that program. It did accept him as a student, but only so many students were allowed into the computer science program each fall, and all the openings for new students in the program were filled. Jawed was not satisfied with the university's decision. Marc Andreessen, one of the creators of the browser software Netscape, had graduated from the university's computer science program. Jawed

A DIVIDED GERMANY

Jawed was born in a country that no longer exists. Germany was divided into East and West following its surrender in World War II in May 1945. From July 17 to August 2, the US, Soviet, and British leaders met to discuss how to deal with Germany's reconstruction. At that time, the nation was divided into four zones for military occupation. Each zone would be overseen by one of the four major Allies: Great Britain in the northwest, France in the southwest, the United States in the southeast, and the Soviet Union in the northeast. Germany's capital, Berlin, was located in the Soviet zone. It was also divided.

The four nations were not harmonious allies. The Communist Soviet Union was led by totalitarian Joseph Stalin, whose beliefs and practices were in direct opposition to those of the three Western powers, particularly the United States. The two nations became bitter rivals.

In May 1949, Germany was officially split into East and West Germany when the Western Allies approved a constitution that created West Germany. East Germany adopted a separate, communism-based constitution. West Germany thrived economically, while East Germany suffered under the tight hold of Soviet communism.

Four decades of division ended when Germany was reunified on October 3, 1990. The Karims lived in West Germany at the time.

wanted to be part of the academic program that produced students like Andreessen.

So Jawed took action. After receiving the unexpected and disappointing letter from the University of Illinois at Urbana-Champaign, Jawed wrote his own letter in return. In it, the young man explained how he was an excellent choice for the program because of his dedication, ambition, and motivation. Jawed's letter made a difference. The school accepted him into the program for the upcoming school year.

HER SON'S LIFE

In a 2006 *New York Times* article, Christine Karim explained her son's interest in technology and learning. She said, "To develop new things and be aware of new things, this is our life."[3]

A CHANGE IN PLANS

In 1997, Karim began his studies at the University of Illinois at Urbana-Champaign as he had hoped and planned. However, an opportunity would arise that would interest Karim so much that he would postpone completing his bachelor's degree.

In 2000, during his junior year, Karim left the computer science program and the university. He

had been offered a job at PayPal, a start-up company
in California. PayPal had been created in March
when Confinity, the creator of PayPal software,
merged with X.com, another Internet business.
Just as had happened during his senior year in high
school for his mother's lab, he would get paid to do
work he loved. But Karim knew the diversion from
his education would not be permanent. A devoted
student, he planned to return to school and complete
his degree at a later time. For now, though, his life
was heading in a different direction. He would meet
others with similar interests and talents in computer
science. While working at PayPal, he would befriend
Steve Chen, another programmer, and Chad Hurley,
a designer. Together, they would develop an idea that
would affect countless computer users around the
world. +

Karim met Chen, *left*, and Hurley, *right*, when he took a job at PayPal in 2000.

Confinity first developed PayPal software for the Palm Pilot.

MEETING AT PAYPAL

By 2000, Steve Chen, Chad Hurley, and Jawed Karim were in their twenties. Each had also moved to the West Coast to take his first job after college—and in the case of Chen and Karim, without finishing their degrees.

The use of computers in homes had grown exponentially since Chen, Hurley, and Karim were born. The boys had grown up using and playing with computers—they were part of one of the earliest generations to do so. Surfing the Internet had become common as the millennium approached, and shopping online was increasing in popularity. But shopping online was not always safe, and users did not want to risk having their credit card numbers taken by online predators. Some creative minds saw the need and possibility for creating technology that would make electronic shopping safer and more secure. PayPal was designed in response to this need.

HOME COMPUTER AND INTERNET USE

The US Census has been tracking the number of computers in US homes since 1984. In 1997, the agency began tracking Internet access as well. In 1997, 18 percent of US households reported having Internet access at home. In 2000, 41.5 reported having Internet access at home. By 2009, that number had jumped to 68.7 percent. The increase in household Internet access and computer use paved the way for YouTube's popularity and growth.

The software known as PayPal was developed by Confinity, founded in December 1998 in Palo Alto, California. Confinity's computing wizards developed software for use with the Palm Pilot, one of the first major handheld devices known as a personal digital assistant (PDA). The software allowed Palm Pilot users to make payments via the Internet using their devices. The company also focused on cryptography, which disguises information to keep it from being stolen.

As more people used electronic devices for making purchases, the need for the security provided by software such as PayPal increased. The software encrypts information, putting it into a code that is not readily available to online thieves looking to steal shoppers' credit card information. PayPal's online payment system expanded to accommodate the growth from PDAs to other forms of electronic purchases, including average people shopping online at home.

EBAY BRINGS CHANGE

The growth and popularity of PayPal did not go unnoticed. In 2002, the online auction company eBay purchased PayPal for $1.5 billion. The secure buying system would fit well with the online auction company's site. By purchasing PayPal, eBay hoped to increase the number of online payments made at the site. This would help the site save money and time by speeding up transactions—processing electronic payments takes less time than processing payments made by cash or check.

eBay's purchase of PayPal sent Hurley's work in a different direction. The change in ownership resulted in bonuses for the employees, including Hurley. Perhaps because the money was enough to free him from having a steady job, or because he simply wanted a change, Hurley left PayPal. He chose to be a consultant in Silicon Valley, the area around Palo Alto and San Francisco that is a center for high-tech companies. He did work for hire for these technology companies. He also started working in other areas. Hurley

EBAY

The now-popular eBay began as Auction-Web in September 1995. Pierre Omidyar, a computer programmer, wrote the initial code for the auction Web site during the Labor Day holiday weekend. Omidyar tested the site by posting a laser pointer up for auction. It was broken, so he was going to throw it away. Surprisingly, he got a bid for the item. Someone bought it for $14.83.

After launching his new business venture, Omidyar hired his first employee in 1996. Chris Agarpao helped manage operations of the company, while Omidyar continued to work for a different company as a full-time employee. A second employee, Jeff Skoll, was hired in 1996 as company president. That year, Omidyar joined his own company as a full-time employee. The company also started making money, earning approximately $5,000 in May and $10,000 in June.

In 1997, AuctionWeb became eBay. That year, the company sold its one-millionth item. The company's initial success continued and increased. As of April 2010, eBay had more than 90 million users. The company had also expanded by purchasing other businesses, including Shopping.com, Bill Me Later, PayPal, and Half.com.

DEDICATED TO SCHOOL

After leaving college to work at PayPal, Karim completed his undergraduate studies online. He earned a bachelor's degree in computer science from the University of Illinois at Urbana-Champaign in 2004.

designed messenger bags—sacks usually worn over one shoulder. He also consulted on the 2005 film *Thank You for Smoking*, which PayPal founder Max Levchin helped finance.

Meanwhile, Karim and Chen continued working at PayPal. Chen worked on launching PayPal in China, a project he focused on for two years. Karim implemented the company's first real-time antifraud system. The software detects illegal activity in PayPal accounts as it happens.

Hurley's departure from PayPal did not end his relationships with Karim and Chen. As employees of a new, small company, they had spent time together at work and become friends.

By 2005, they would all be former employees of PayPal. They would also become partners in a new venture. Their collaboration would result in a creation that would quickly change how computer users experience the Internet and connect with other Internet users worldwide. +

After leaving PayPal, Hurley consulted on the movie *Thank You for Smoking*, starring Aaron Eckhart, *above*.

Chen, Karim, and Hurley had an idea for a Web site that would make sharing home videos easier.

"BROADCAST YOURSELF"

In 2005, Chen, Hurley, and Karim were working together once again, but not at PayPal. They had decided to join forces to create something new. All three men had achieved success in the dot-com world of computer-based business and wanted to use their knowledge, skills, and experience to continue working with technology. They loved the possibilities the Internet offered and simply needed to find just the right idea to pursue as a team.

THE IDEA

One story of the idea for YouTube explains that Chen and Hurley had been to a dinner party with friends. During the party, guests captured the evening with digital photographs and video. The photos could easily be e-mailed or uploaded to the Internet for the friends to share with one another. Sharing the video, however, presented a challenge.

Another story involves two events that both captured the attention of the world, but for very different reasons. The first had happened during Janet Jackson's halftime performance during Super Bowl XXXVIII in February 2004—she had a mishap with her costume resulting in inadvertent nudity. The other event was the 2004 Indian Ocean tsunami. The natural disaster had claimed thousands of lives in Southeast Asia in December. Both news stories had been covered by television and cable networks, but finding footage of the events online was difficult.

Regardless of where the idea came from, what matters is that Chen, Hurley, and Karim saw a need: there had to be a way to make it easier to put—and find—videos online. It was something they were interested in personally. They assumed other computer users had to be interested as well. And with the constant advances in computers, Internet service, and access, the three men could capitalize on technology to make their idea a reality.

Chen, Hurley, and Karim decided to create a video-sharing Web site. They debated what kind of video site they would create. An early version focused on dating. It was named Tune In Hook Up, and its idea came from another popular site, Hot or Not, which allowed users to rate the attractiveness of the people who uploaded their pictures to the site. But the three creators decided Tune In Hook Up was too limited in focus and continued to work on their idea.

Keeping the focus on videos, the three men then created a site for hosting videos for online auctions. The site was still undergoing testing— or what is called the beta phase of software development—in spring 2005. Eventually, the three young entrepreneurs determined the site did not have to focus on a single type of video, such as those created to get a date or to sell an item. Rather, their site could be a platform for all kinds of videos.

LAUNCHING YOUTUBE

Chen, Hurley, and Karim pressed on, collaborating to design a site they themselves would use and that others would likely use as well. The trio needed a place to work, so they created an office in Hurley's garage. They also needed supplies and computer equipment. Another expense was power and data storage space. The Web site needed enough bandwidth to keep the site from crashing if hundreds or thousands of users accessed it at the same time. Transferring data requires bandwidth, and the more bandwidth

YOUTUBE'S TECHNOLOGY

One of the factors contributing to YouTube's high start-up and maintenance costs is the site's need for a high bandwidth and ample storage space. Both of these are critical to YouTube's ability to function. Storage space allows the site to house its millions of videos. Bandwidth (amount and rate of data transfer) allows simultaneous viewing of videos by millions of users without crashing the site.

Chen was paying for much of YouTube's costs and had maxed out his credit cards. Chen called PayPal's Max Levchin for help, saying, "The servers are running too hot. We need more servers, and we need to get more money."[1] Levchin referred Chen and his partners to Sequoia Capital, a company that provides money to companies to help them launch and succeed. In addition to providing funding to YouTube and PayPal, the California-based business has also helped Apple, LinkedIn, Yahoo!, and Zappos.com.

New technology changed the way users access the Internet, including video-sharing sites such as YouTube.

the site had, the more successful it would be. Initial expenses were taken care of by Chen, who paid for a lot of the start-up costs using his credit cards.

With work space, data storage space, and materials acquired, the entrepreneurs could get to work bringing their idea to life. Each of the men focused on tasks he was good at. Hurley used his design skills to create the interface, or look of the site, and a logo. Chen and Karim focused on the technical aspects.

Technology and design were major concerns for the entrepreneurs. The site had to be simple. Users were not going to have to buy or download software to use the site. They wanted anyone to be able to use it. Users also would not need a degree in computer science or a lot of computer know-how to take advantage of the site. At the start, the three men wanted to get the site up and running and were not as concerned about using it to make money. However, YouTube had to balance ease of use with technical quality. In some cases, the quality suffered—such as video resolution—but this would be something the founders would address.

With these basic concerns covered, Chen, Hurley, and Karim had to think about the site's name. On February 15, 2005, the trio decided to make their venture official. They established the company YouTube LLC and registered a domain name: YouTube.com. They eventually settled on a motto for their company and site: Broadcast Yourself. The men had created a site for users to share their videos, and the motto encouraged visitors to be creative.

By spring, YouTube.com was up and running with a test version of the site. At this point, the

UTUBE.COM

Many computer seekers of YouTube mistakenly searched for utube.com. The influx of users was a problem for the site utube.com—the site simply could not handle so many people accessing it at once. This site belonged to Universal Tube & Rollform Equipment Corporation, a company in Ohio that makes pipes, tubes, and other machinery. The company changed its Web address to utubeonline.com to remedy the problem.

YOUTUBE'S SECOND VIDEO

The second video posted on YouTube was "My Snowboard Skillz." It was added to the site on April 23, 2005, the same day as "Me at the zoo," YouTube's first video. The ten-second video shows a person snowboarding onto and falling off a small ramp.

functionality was limited, but the site was usable. The site's first video was posted on April 23, 2005. "Me at the zoo" featured Karim. The 18-second video was taken at a zoo and showed the computer whiz standing in front of an elephant exhibit. Karim said in the video, "All right, so here we are in front of the elephants. The cool thing about these guys is that they have really, really, really long trunks, and that's, that's cool. And that's pretty much all there is to say."[2] Although the video itself was not elaborate, its posting was a successful test of YouTube's video-sharing capability and reflected a new cultural interest in sharing quiet, everyday events through video. With the first video posted, the designer and computer programmers kept working to improve their creation.

YOUTUBE CATCHES ON

As with the owners of any new business, Chen, Hurley, and Karim brainstormed ideas for attracting people to their site. Thinking about how many computer users and technology geeks were young men, they thought getting videos featuring attractive women would help. The trio came up with a plan that would use another popular Web site. Chen, Hurley, and Karim posted an advertisement on Craigslist's Los Angeles site. The Web site allowed them to advertise for free. In addition, computer users well beyond the city limits could find that ad, which explained that beautiful women would be paid $100 to post ten videos of themselves on YouTube. The ad was not successful. No one responded to it.

The men kept tweaking YouTube. In June 2005, four new features were added. After a user finished watching a video, one feature provided recommendations of other videos related or similar to the one just watched. A second feature would allow a user to e-mail a friend about a video with a single click. A third provided for user interaction by allowing comments on videos. The last provided an external video player that allowed YouTube videos to be posted to other Web sites, such as MySpace. With a simple copy and paste, users were now able to add their videos to their social networking Web pages to share with anyone they wanted.

These changes helped launch YouTube's popularity, and the site started catching on. Karim's

FORM AND FUNCTION

Not everyone has good things to say about YouTube's design and capability. A report published by Paula Alexandra Silva and Alan Dix from the United Kingdom's Lancaster University gave a negative review to YouTube's design. They claimed the site is visually cluttered and chaotic. Many people have also complained about the low quality of YouTube videos. Writer Josh Lowensohn compared YouTube to four other video-hosting sites: Vimeo, Facebook, Veoh, and Viddler. Both Viddler and Facebook were faster at uploading videos.

"Me at the zoo" was joined by thousands of other videos. Initially, users posted videos of themselves and their home movies. Television commercials from Europe were also popular—US viewers were attracted to their less conservative style.

The increase in use and popularity proved helpful in obtaining financing. In November 2005, Chen, Hurley, and Karim received $3.5 million in backing for their online venture from Sequoia Capital, a company that had once helped PayPal. With the much-needed funds to help keep their dream going, the three creators kept moving forward. In December, YouTube officially launched its Web site. YouTube.com was no longer in its testing phase. Internet users worldwide would quickly make it an Internet phenomenon. +

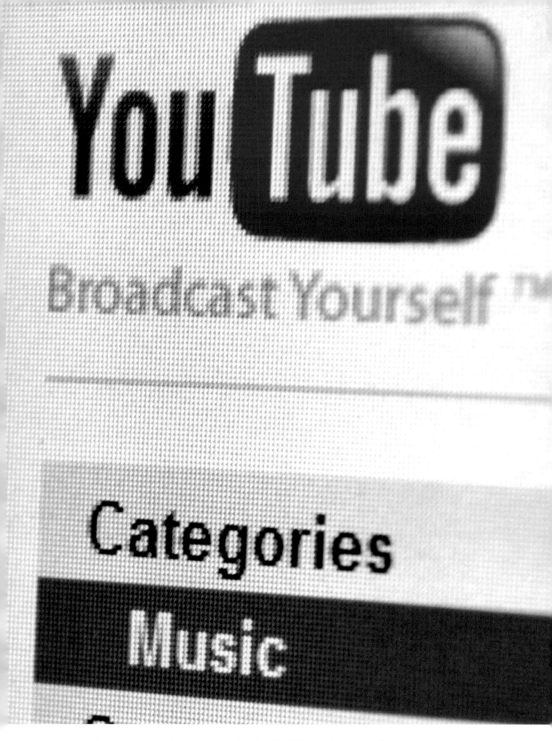

Some users and designers criticize YouTube's design for lacking a unified theme.

Facebook founder Mark Zuckerberg

SOCIAL IMPACT

A round the same time that YouTube was getting started, other social networking sites were also growing in popularity. Facebook, MySpace, and blog sites such as Xanga and LiveJournal allowed users to create profiles and share words, photos, and—with the help of YouTube—videos with the world. MySpace and Facebook users could embed or link to YouTube videos on their profiles, so as those sites grew, so did YouTube.

The increase in YouTube's popularity brought growth in the company and a need for more money. In April 2006, YouTube received more funding from Sequoia Capital. This time, the amount was $8 million. The additional backing allowed the company to move out of Hurley's garage. Operations were moved to office space above a pizzeria in nearby San Mateo, California, and the company hired its first employees, which totaled around 20. Hurley became chief executive officer and oversaw management of the company and its business matters. Chen was made chief technology officer at YouTube.

Karim, however, did not want a title, a salary, or the benefits that employees usually have. Rather than become an employee, Karim acted as an adviser. And by the time the company received its second round of funding from Sequoia Capital, he had decided to go back to school. He had been accepted into a graduate program in computer science at Stanford University in nearby Palo Alto, California. Karim was not far away if Chen

KARIM LEAVES

Sequoia Capital's Roelof Botha said of keeping Karim at YouTube, "I wish we could have kept him as part of the company. He was very, very creative."[1]

and Hurley wanted his input. The two men and their new employees continued moving forward.

The young executives worked well together. Hurley's artistic abilities and Chen's technological savvy seemed to be a winning combination. Hurley's friend and former colleague Ryan Donahue said of Hurley, "He is sort of an anomaly. Because if you look at the successful start-up stories, the formulaic founders' team is usually an engineer and a business person, or two engineers. It's rarely a designer or a truly creative person."[2] But Hurley was a creative person, and YouTube was a success.

YOUTUBE'S APPEAL

YouTube is appealing because it is easy to use. Searching for videos is similar to searching with Google. Users can simply type a few words in the search field to sort through the videos available for viewing. The site also has more than a dozen categories for browsing, including comedy, entertainment, music, and sports. To watch a video, a user needs only to click play. For users who want to upload a video, the action is similar to attaching a file to an e-mail. However, YouTube does limit the sizes of files uploaded to the site.

Another appealing aspect of YouTube is its price for users. Whether viewing or uploading, the cost is nothing. In addition, registration is not required to view YouTube's offerings. For those who want to upload videos, registration is simple. Users create an account by selecting a user name and providing their location (country), zip code, date of birth, and gender.

In addition to being easy to use and free, YouTube is more than a site for viewing videos. The four features added to YouTube in June 2005 really prompted the Web site's success. Visitors could share videos with family and friends—and the world. They could share their thoughts on the videos they watched by adding comments that other users could read and also respond to. These updates made

YOUTUBE CHANNELS

One method for browsing YouTube videos is by channel. As with categories, YouTube offers several channel selections, including those of comedians, directors, musicians, politicians, and reporters. In *YouTube 4 You*, Michael Miller explained channels:

On YouTube, a channel is just a fancy name for a user's profile. Other users can access your channel/profile to find out what videos you've uploaded and which videos are your favorites; you can also subscribe to a user's profile to be notified when the user uploads new videos to the YouTube site.[3]

Each channel has a main page from which users navigate. Some channel pages are quite simple, with a white or solid-color background and few graphics. Partner channels often have more complex designs if they belong to commercial partners such as television networks, music companies, and athletic associations.

Each channel reflects the owner's personality—within certain YouTube-required limits—through its design style and the videos available on the page. And it provides a readily available place for friends, family, and fans to view videos created or selected by the channel owner.

the site more of a community for some and boosted the number of visitors.

VIDEO REPOSITORY

YouTube is essentially a video repository. For the many people worldwide who record home videos, YouTube provides an easy way to share their creations with family and friends without having to deal with the long transfer times that sending videos via e-mail can take. For users who are more serious about their videos and focused on the art of filmmaking, YouTube serves as a sounding board. In addition to being able to share videos with friends and family members, these users can essentially create an easily accessible online portfolio of videos for potential employers. And these participants can use the site as a means for getting feedback on their work. Video posters can read the comments by those who have watched their creations and, ideally, receive valuable criticism.

For those who love to watch videos, YouTube has millions available, and they can be watched with a simple click of a button. The new videos uploaded daily highlight posters' personal lives, talents, and interests. And not all videos are new. Videos of older television programs and performances are available.

The site can help visitors keep up with current events as well, as many videos capture what is happening in the world. For example, when Haiti experienced an earthquake in 2010 that caused massive damage, injuries, and death, people worldwide were immediately able to view footage of the aftermath. A few hours after the quake, the Red Cross posted an update on the disaster on YouTube. Viewers could watch Tracy Reines, the director of Response Operations for the American Red Cross, as she discussed the latest in disaster response. The YouTube post also provided information about donating to the relief efforts. This experience sharply contrasted to that of the 2004 Indian Ocean tsunami, when videos of the event could not be found online. YouTube helped spread video sharing through the Internet. The world's events—big and small—had become easily accessible by computer users worldwide.

A YOUTUBE STAR

Not surprisingly, the growth in the number and variety of videos and viewers has led to YouTube favorites. YouTube has its own celebrities. By the summer of 2006, just months

MASSIVE AMOUNTS OF DATA

In June 2007, the British Broadcasting Corporation (BBC) reported, "In one day, YouTube sends the data equivalent of 75 billion e-mails."[4]

after the site officially launched, YouTube had created one of its first stars.

Brooke Brodack was a hostess at a restaurant in Massachusetts when YouTube launched. Not long after she began posting videos to the site, she was recognized in public, including at her workplace, as Brookers—her online name. YouTube viewers first saw Brookers in October 2005, when she posted "Crazed Numa Fan!!!!" In this parody of another YouTube video, "Numa Numa Dance" by Gary Brolsma, Brooke—and, sometimes, her sister—lip-synch and dance to a song by O-Zone, a band from Moldova. Brooke puts her all into the performance, going wild with her dancing as she sings "Dragostea Din Tei."

Brodack created the film using a computer, a camcorder, and moviemaking software. Brodack posted additional videos in other styles on her YouTube channel, or profile. In one film, she discussed why children eat glue. In another, she staged a short commercial for coffee. Viewers liked what they saw and continued to watch what the young woman uploaded. She became so popular that Hollywood took notice. In June 2006, Brodack signed an 18-month contract with Carson Daly, a late-night talk show host, who saw and liked "Crazed

Numa Fan!!!!" He said of Brodack, "She has a voice, she has an opinion, she's crazy, and I couldn't stop watching her."[5]

Shortly after signing Brodack to an 18-month contract, Carson Daly launched the Web project, It's Your Show. The project awarded cash to users who contributed videos to the site that were judged as being the best. Brodack helped develop content for the site.

STATISTICS

Like Daly, YouTube viewers could not stop watching Brookers, nor the many other broadcasters who posted their creations daily. From its formal launch in December 2005, the number of people visiting YouTube grew almost monthly. The number of unique visitors increased. In addition to having repeat users, first-time users continued to visit and explore the site.

By summer 2006, YouTube had become a major online presence and captured the top spot for online video. YouTube had a larger share of the market than competitors Yahoo!, MSN, Google, and AOL combined. These competitors highlighted services different from those of

"Our goal is to have YouTube on every screen—to take it from the PC to the living room and the mobile phone."[6]
—Steve Chen, YouTube cofounder

YouTube's focus. Google was the go-to search engine, MSN offered news, and Yahoo! and AOL served as portals to massive amounts of information on the Web. But none of these focused solely on delivering videos, and YouTube's single-minded attention to video sharing showed. At the time, YouTube videos accounted for 60 percent of all online videos. In June 2006, 2.5 billion videos were watched, with more than 65,000 videos uploaded to the site every day.

YouTube's growth in popularity seemed exponential. This growth required more money if the site was to continue to succeed. YouTube required a lot of funding to create and maintain. The site was earning some income from advertising revenue, but it had the potential to earn much more—especially with its ever-increasing number of viewers. This earning potential was not lost on another major dot-com, which would soon become YouTube's owner. +

Brooke Brodack, *standing*, attended a press event in October 2010 to talk about a new Comedy Central television project.

Hurley and Chen pose for a photo with their laptops in 2006 following the sale of YouTube to Google.

SOLD!

Within a few months of its official launch in December 2005, YouTube was an online hit. That month, records showed that 3,105,000 different users visited YouTube. In January 2006, almost 5 million unique visitors accessed the site, and by February, the number grew to more than 9 million unique visitors. In May, there were more than 20 million unique visitors, and in July, there were more than 30 million. YouTube was a rising star, and the site seemed poised to only keep growing.

CHALLENGES

As YouTube grew in popularity, it caught the eye of people in the technology community. But the site had a problem: it cost a lot to maintain and was not bringing in a lot of revenue—at least not nearly enough to keep the business going. With the constant increase in traffic, the site required more and more bandwidth and storage space, which were not cheap.

Increasing advertising could bring in much-needed revenue, but the company was concerned about balancing advertising with the general user experience. The continuous addition of videos also posed challenges to the company. One challenge YouTube has faced and continues to address is appropriateness of content. The site has been criticized repeatedly for inappropriate content. Because users upload content, a variety of material becomes available on the site. Not all users find all material acceptable. For example, some videos include violence, animal cruelty, foul language, or nudity. And some content is not suitable for children.

In May 2006, a *Fortune* magazine reporter asked Chen and Hurley about keeping the site's content suitable for all viewers. The two men explained the process:

> **Hurley:** *Well, we say no nudity, obscenity, profanity, or violence.*
>
> **Chen:** *More important, it's the community of users themselves. They feel like they've built it up, so they want to try to keep it clean. They let us know when there's content that shouldn't be there, and we take it down.*[1]

As Chen noted, YouTube users flag questionable content. YouTube is then responsible for removing it. YouTube is constantly changing—not just as videos are added but also as questionable videos are removed. But this process can cause frustration as users navigate the site looking for videos that had previously been there. It also makes YouTube a somewhat unreliable video repository.

In addition to inappropriate material, copyright issues emerged early in the company's life. Copyright grants a person or an organization legal ownership of an original work, such as a movie, video, song, or book. Copyright laws exist to protect unauthorized use of such works, and the copyright holder can sue when his or her material is used without permission.

In December 2005, YouTube faced this very issue. A user had recorded the popular television show *Saturday Night Live* on December 17 and uploaded part of the program to the video-sharing site. The skit "Lazy Sunday: The Chronicles of

YOUTUBE AWARDS

In March 2007, YouTube presented its first awards for videos posted on its site. The winners included:

- **Most Creative:** "Here It Goes Again." This music video by OK Go features the band's four members performing a choreographed dance on eight moving treadmills.

- **Best Series:** "Ask a Ninja." Created by comedians Kent Nichols and Douglas Sarine, the series features a ninja in black garb answering e-mails using ninja vocabulary and jokingly signing off with "I look forward to killing you soon."[2]

- **Best Comedy:** "Smosh." Created by Anthony Padilla and Ian Hecox, known also as Smosh, the college students had the second-most-subscribed channel on YouTube at the time.

- **Best Music:** "Terranaomi." Created by Terra Naomi, the exposure brought by YouTube helped the singer get a music contract with Island Records.

- **Most Adorable Video:** "Kiwi." Computer animator Dony Permedi shares the experiences of a kiwi bird trying to fly.

Narnia" became a YouTube hit. However, NBC, the television network that broadcasts *Saturday Night Live*, owns the material. NBC learned about the popular YouTube video and promptly asked the site to remove the illegal footage. YouTube obliged, posting an explanation on its blog: "NBC recently contacted YouTube and asked us to remove 'Saturday Night Live's' 'Lazy Sunday: Chronicles of Narnia' video. We know how popular that video is, but YouTube respects the rights of copyright holders."[3]

YouTube has taken steps to make sure its users have information about copyright and the consequences of copyright infringement. On the YouTube site, links are provided to other sites with information about US copyright law. But ultimately, YouTube users are responsible for educating themselves. YouTube encourages users to avoid copyright issues by creating completely original material. And this very material is what gives YouTube its unique identity.

Chen and Hurley continued to face the challenges of owning and operating YouTube. But YouTube would soon deal with some of its copyright issues through strategic and influential partnerships.

The band OK Go won most creative video for its music video "Here It Goes Again" in the first YouTube Video Awards in 2007.

AN OFFER THEY COULD NOT REFUSE

Chen and Hurley's work did not go unnoticed. YouTube garnered increasing attention by the media. It also caught the eye of Google. The well-known and well-used search engine saw YouTube's potential and made Chen and Hurley an offer they simply could not refuse.

In October 2006, the two young executives announced in a video on their own site that Google was buying YouTube. On October 9, 2006, Google

Each year, *Time* magazine names a person of the year. This is usually someone who made a tremendous impact during the previous year. The publication did something quite different for 2006. *Time* selected "you." The change reflected the growth of the Web. Reporter Lev Grossman wrote, "It's a story about community and collaboration on a scale never seen before. It's about the cosmic compendium of knowledge Wikipedia and the million-channel people's network YouTube and the online metropolis MySpace. It's about the many wresting power from the few and helping one another for nothing and how that will not only change the world, but also change the way the world changes."[4]

purchased YouTube for $1.65 billion in stock. The announcement came on the heels of other YouTube deals. Earlier that day, Chen and Hurley revealed three additional business deals. YouTube had entered into separate agreements with three media companies—CBS Corporation, Sony BMG Music Entertainment, and Universal Music Group—to allow their music videos to be watched on YouTube. All three companies had experienced copyright infringement as a result of YouTube. Under the new deal, the music companies would allow their copyrighted music videos on YouTube in exchange for shared revenue generated from advertisements. Warner Music Group had also experienced copyright violations because of the Web site and had agreed to a similar partnership a few weeks earlier. With these major copyright issues resolved as a result of the partnerships, Google and YouTube finalized their agreement.

YouTube's third founder, Jawed Karim, was not part of the deal-making process. He explained his role in and noted thoughts about the history-making business agreement, "My only interest was in helping the company get off the ground, implementing it, and raising money. I definitely thought that this was a possible outcome. But I didn't think it was the most likely outcome."[5]

GOOGLE

Google became such a popular search engine that it was added to *Merriam-Webster's Collegiate Dictionary* as a verb in 2006. The definition of *google* is "to use the Google search engine to obtain information about [various subject matter] on the World Wide Web."[6]

PURCHASING POSSIBILITY

Buying YouTube did not provide Google with immediate revenue. It simply could not, because the video-sharing Web site was not profitable. In mid-2006, news sources speculated that YouTube, despite its immense popularity, was losing money at a rate of $500,000 per month. Rather, the purchase was about advertising possibility. Charlene Li is an analyst with Forrester Research, a company that specializes in technology and marketing research. She said of Google's purchase, "This gives Google the video play they have been looking for and gives them a great opportunity to redefine how advertising is done."[7]

Ultimately, the site could prove quite lucrative for Google. With so many page views, the search-engine pioneer could sell advertising on YouTube's Web pages, earning money each time a user accesses a page that has an ad on it. Each time a page appears to a viewer, an ad loads with it. This single appearance of an ad is an impression. A single advertisement can be placed on YouTube's home page and charged per 1,000 impressions, which is common in Web advertising (it is known as CPM: cost per thousand). For example, 1,000 ad impressions (1 CPM) could cost ten dollars. If the site has 30 million visitors to its home page a day, an ad would be shown 30 million times. Since advertising is sold per thousand impressions, dividing the 30 million impressions by 1,000 (1 CPM)

HURLEY'S GOOD FORTUNE

Hurley's former roommate Ryan Donahue spoke of Hurley's successful career. Donahue said, "Either he was incredibly brilliant and he saw the opportunity, or he was really lucky—I don't know. But to hit gold with your first job out of college is pretty rare. And then for his first company to be YouTube, he's gotta be a smart guy."[8]

would equal 30,000 CPMs. At a cost of ten dollars per CPM, this ad on YouTube would generate $300,000 in revenue in one day, a considerable sum.

Videos themselves are another advertising possibility. With so many popular videos, space in the video can also be sold. With viral videos getting millions of views, Google could potentially earn millions of dollars from a single video. Google put these options into practice, but in 2009, news sources reported that YouTube was still unable to turn a profit. Numbers varied widely, but some estimates showed that bandwidth expenses for the site cost approximately $1 million per day. With such high operating costs, YouTube would need to overcome some serious challenges in becoming a profitable venture.

For Chen, Hurley, and Karim, however, significant earnings from YouTube had become a reality. Selling their creation to Google netted the three young men millions of dollars. Karim received approximately $66 million in Google stock. This amount was only a fraction of that earned by Chen and Hurley, who each received more than $300 million worth of Google stock in the deal. Hurley spoke about the deal in terms of technological possibility, saying, "I'm confident that with this partnership we'll have the flexibility and resources needed to pursue our goal of building the next-generation platform for serving media worldwide."[9] Indeed, they would. +

YouTube sensation Terra Naomi went on to get a contract with Island Records.

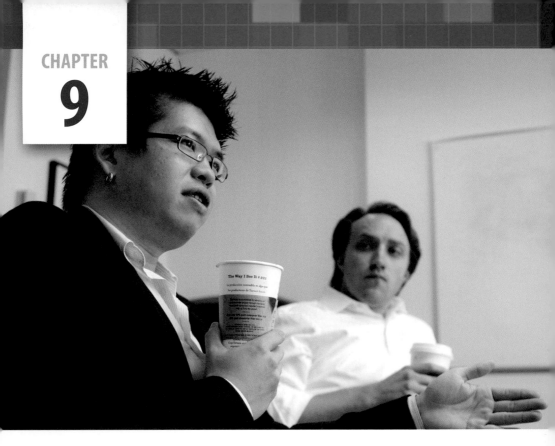

Chen and Hurley talk with an interviewer in 2007.

NEW OWNER, SAME YOUTUBE

Wenhile company buyouts often result in employees leaving the business, Chen and Hurley did not give up their positions at YouTube after selling their company to Google. Hurley remained the chief executive officer, while Chen continued to work as YouTube's chief technology officer. The change in ownership would not deter users from visiting the popular site. Instead, as had been the case since YouTube's launch, the number of people accessing the site continued to increase.

THE POPULAR BECOME PARTNERS

The year 2007 saw a change in YouTube's partners. The site expanded its partners to include more than those from the commercial realm, such as CBS and the British Broadcasting Corporation (BBC). Instead, some of YouTube's most popular users were made partners. On May 3, 2007, YouTube explained its partnership program for those who create original content and post to the site. These user-partners would be able to make money from advertisements that appear next to their original videos, much like YouTube's corporate partners.

In 2008, the *New York Times* reported on the success of the program for some YouTube enthusiasts, known as YouTubers:

> One year after YouTube, the online video powerhouse, invited members to become "partners" and added advertising to their videos, the most successful users are earning six-figure incomes from the Web site.[1]

"What we're really excited about . . . is that literally, at any given moment, thousands of creative people from throughout the world are posting new, original content to YouTube. It's this community that's shaping what the YouTube experience is now and will be in the future, and we're incredibly excited for the prospect that holds."[2]

—*YouTube.com, announcing its user-partner program in 2007*

Michael Buckley is one computer user who is capitalizing on YouTube's partner program. An original user-partner, Buckley and a few others were invited by YouTube to be a partner before the program was opened to everyone. Buckley quit his job as an administrative assistant when his YouTube earnings surpassed what he earned from his job. But the earnings were not immediate. The host of a weekly online show that highlights entertainment gossip in a humorous way, Buckley worked full-time—40 hours per week—on YouTube before he made any money.

Cory Williams is another successful YouTube user-partner. With subscribers to his channel numbering 180,000 in 2008, Williams claimed earnings of $17,000 to $20,000 per month. Williams explained that half of the money came from advertisements and half came from sponsorships— just as feature films make money from product placement, so does Williams. In June 2010, Williams's subscribers numbered more than 420,000.

ADVANCED COPYRIGHT POLICIES

From its beginning, YouTube has faced copyright issues. Pirated audio and video often ended up on the site. Business deals with select major media companies in October 2006—in conjunction with the sale to Google—avoided copyright lawsuits by these companies, but they have not prevented all copyright infringements. To combat this issue, YouTube created tools and policies that better honor rights holders and help them manage how their content is used.

YouTube developed Audio ID and Video ID to help address the issue of piracy. The feature allows copyright holders to identify videos that contain all or part of their copyrighted content. Once videos with pirated material are identified, the copyright holder can choose what happens to the videos. This gives the copyright holder control of his or her content. Each copyright holder can choose whether he or she wants the material monetized, tracked, or blocked. Monetizing happens through YouTube's partner program, in which user-partners earn money through advertising revenue. Tracking allows the copyright holder to see how the content is being used and viewed, which could potentially increase fan interaction and provide access to market data that could help earn money. Or, the automated system could remove the video with pirated material entirely. However, some users are skeptical about how well the system identifies pirated material.

Advertising began appearing with videos as a result of this feature. For example, the popular wedding video posted by newlyweds Kevin Heinz and Jill Peterson featured the couple's wedding party dancing down the aisle to Chris Brown's song "Forever." The video page has links to a Chris Brown YouTube page, as well as Amazon and iTunes, where users can purchase the song.

YOUTUBE: THE NUMBERS

As YouTube has gained popularity and fame, its numbers have increased dramatically. The amount of content the site has and the frequency of its use can be understood using a variety of numbers.

On May 23, 2010, Emma Barnett reported the following details about YouTube in her article "Top 10 Facts You didn't know about YouTube":

- **45,000,000:** *The number of hits YouTube's homepage receives daily.*

- **1,000,000:** *In September 2005, Brazilian soccer star Ronaldinho's Nike ad "Touch of Gold" became the first YouTube video to be seen 1 million times.*

- **1,700:** *The number of years it would take to watch every YouTube video.*

- **100:** *The number of years of video scanned daily by YouTube's content ID technology.*

- **70:** *The percentage of non-U.S. users visiting YouTube.*

- **24:** *The number of hours of video added to YouTube every minute.*

- **15:** *The average number of minutes a user spends on YouTube daily.[3]*

TALENT POOL

Kevin Heinz and Jill Peterson are just two of YouTube's many stars. Since the launch of Brooke Brodack—Brookers—as a YouTube celebrity in 2005, other YouTube users worldwide have gained popularity on the site. And some have been discovered online.

In 2007, Dutch teenager Esmee Denters was considering offers from US record companies who had seen homemade videos of her singing on YouTube. Pop superstar Justin Bieber was discovered after he posted homemade videos of himself singing. On July 16, 2010, his video for "Baby" became the most-viewed YouTube video ever with 246 million views.

YOUTUBE GATHERINGS

In addition to being discovered online, some users have discovered each other offline. In February 2007, some 100 video bloggers (or vloggers) attended "As One." The event in San Francisco was planned to bring together YouTube's most popular bloggers.

In September 2007, more than 150 YouTubers gathered near Washington DC. Some traveled from as far as California to attend. One participant described the experience: "These are people we

---

SAFETY CENTER

YouTube is committed to building a community, and the site offers online safety advice. YouTube's Safety Center page provides the following quick tips:

- "Flag videos that violate our Community Guidelines.
- "Keep personal videos private.
- "Block users whose comments or messages are bothering you.
- "Keep comments clean and respectful."[5]

---

see for two and a half minutes online every day, and now all of the sudden I can poke them and touch them and see they're real. It's beautiful."[4]

YouTube meet-ups happen all over the world. Anthropologist Patricia G. Lange, a researcher at the University of Southern California, has attended meet-ups in Los Angeles, Minneapolis, New York City, Philadelphia, Toronto, and other cities. YouTube's site gives details on meet-up groups.

BLOCKED ACCESS

But not everyone is enthusiastic about YouTube. Appropriateness of content has been an ongoing issue. Often, it was on a small level, such as parents concerned about what their children were watching on the site. In the late 2000s, the issue grew in scope to include schools and entire countries, some of which blocked access to the popular Web site.

By 2007, six of Australia's eight states had blocked YouTube in their schools. Cyberbullying had become a major concern. Cyberbullying is the use of digital technology and cell phones—usually by young people—to abuse others. This can be done through harassment, embarrassment, and threats. Schools wanted to end its spread. A video of a humiliating attack on a teenage girl had been posted on YouTube. The public was outraged.

In addition, users can post hurtful or profane comments on other users' videos. Content simply could not be controlled. Australia's Queensland Education and Training Minister Rod Welford explained, "The website was considered unsafe because it was impossible to determine what sort of video material might be accessed by students."[6]

Several nations have blocked YouTube, leaving citizens and visitors alike unable to access the site. In 2007, Thailand blocked the site after a video making fun of its king was uploaded. Also, Morocco blocked the site, leaving some to wonder if the government was trying to control the media by limiting access to information that Moroccan newspapers and television stations were not allowed to report. China also blocked the Web site in an effort to stop citizens from seeing riots that had taken place in the city of Ürümqi in July 2009.

"YouTube is a platform, a distribution vehicle. We don't produce content but we give content creators the ability to reach an audience perhaps they weren't able to reach before—perhaps they didn't have distribution or syndication vehicles to reach the audience. We have upload mechanisms to mass upload files and tools to create branded channels."[7]

—Steve Chen, in a 2007 interview with BBC News

Other nations have blocked YouTube for religious reasons. In early 2008, Pakistan stopped citizens from accessing the site because of content deemed offensive to Islam, a religion many Pakistanis practice. In May 2010, YouTube became one of approximately 450 Web sites the nation blocked because of content it considered objectionable. Given the array of beliefs in the world and the variety of videos available on YouTube, appropriateness of content will likely be an ongoing issue. Nevertheless, what also seems likely to continue is the site's growth and popularity. +

Hurley speaks about emerging social network models and the changing Internet at the World Economic Forum in Switzerland in 2007.

Democratic presidential candidates answered questions delivered via YouTube videos during a 2008 debate.

POLITICS, POP MUSIC, AND BEYOND

F rom the launch of its beta version in spring 2005, YouTube has worked to create a site—a service, really—that allows viewers to express themselves in myriad ways. It is a platform for learning, for being entertained, for keeping up with current events, for sharing important personal events, and even for informing voters.

INFLUENCING VOTERS

In 2007, British prime minister Tony Blair became the first world leader with a YouTube channel. And in 2008, US politicians took advantage of the innovative Web site to reach voters during the campaign leading up to the November presidential election.

Republican and Democratic presidential hopefuls created their own channels on YouTube. Christian Ferry worked for Senator John McCain as his eCampaign director in 2008. Ferry said of the Web site:

> *YouTube provides a unique opportunity to connect directly with voters. The ability for voters to give direct, unfiltered feedback and insight into the issues that matter most to them is an invaluable asset to the Senator.*[1]

The popular Web site created an election-centered initiative named YouTube You Choose '08. It featured material designed to educate voters, including campaign videos and speeches, informal chats, and behind-the-scenes footage. Hurley explained YouTube's role in the 2008 election:

Online video has quickly become an essential way for the general public to become politically informed and empowered. At its core, YouTube is about democracy and self-expression and we're proud to be providing politicians with an environment where they can share information with voters.[2]

FIVEYEAR CHANNEL

YouTube has always been focused on providing users a platform for sharing. And in 2010, YouTube celebrated its fifth anniversary of offering that service. In honor of the event, Google launched YouTube—FiveYear Channel. The anniversary site includes a timeline of its first five years and playlists compiled by celebrity curators, including journalist and news anchor Katie Couric and comedian Conan O'Brien.

The special site also includes "My YouTube Story," which asks users to share how YouTube has affected them. By early October, more than 7 million videos were uploaded to the special anniversary site. The channel's home page features a mosaic of still images from some of these videos.

YouTube's influence is undeniable. Regular people have become household names, if only for a few minutes. Pop singers' music videos have gone viral and increased the performers' popularity. Current events including political campaigns have been viewed and reviewed.

MOVING FORWARD

YouTube has changed owners and undergone some changes since it started. Perhaps the most noticeable was in spring 2010, when a new, simpler design was launched. Despite numerous changes, YouTube still retains its basic functions, which include uploading,

ACTIONS SPEAK LOUDER THAN WORDS

In June 2010, a New York district judge ruled in favor of Google in a copyright infringement case filed against the company in 2007 by Viacom. During YouTube's first two years, thousands of YouTube videos featured content from Viacom's stations, which include MTV and Nickelodeon. Viacom sued Google in 2007 for more than $1 billion in damages from copyright violations.

In his decision, the judge noted YouTube's actions in addressing the issue. On February 2, 2007, Viacom had sent YouTube a list of approximately 100,000 videos that needed to be removed from the site. YouTube removed almost all of the videos by the next business day.

Some of the lawsuit's controversy stemmed from interpretation of the Digital Millennium Copyright Act (DMCA), which was revised in 1998 in order to address new copyright concerns brought about by emerging technologies and information-sharing methods. Viacom believed that YouTube had violated the terms of the DMCA. In 2010, exemptions were made to the DMCA, including relaxed regulations for those who use short clips from DVDs in their own noncommercial videos.

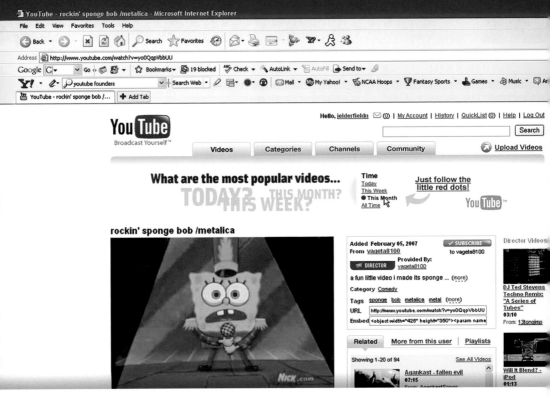

The Spongebob character, owned by Viacom, was seen on YouTube in 2007. Viacom sued YouTube and Google for widespread copyright infringement.

viewing, and commenting on videos. Users of varying abilities, interests, and backgrounds continue to use the site in ever-increasing numbers. In spring 2010, the site was up to 2 billion views per day.

At the time of YouTube's fifth anniversary, Hurley commented on the site he helped create, saying, "Our biggest challenge is making sure we don't taste too many things."[3] In other words, the site has to be careful not to try to do too much or spread itself in too many directions. Hurley went on to explain that social networking was becoming a focus for the site.

And YouTube will undoubtedly continue to focus on challenges. Audio ID and Video ID and agreements with industry giants such as Sony have helped address YouTube's longstanding issues with copyright infringement. However, content appropriateness continues to be an ongoing criticism.

CHEN, HURLEY, AND KARIM

Since selling their creation to Google in 2006, Chen, Hurley, and Karim have continued working in technology. Chen stayed with YouTube following its change in ownership. He remained the site's chief technology officer until fall 2008. At that time, he stepped down from the role. But as of June 2009, he was working with Google on some of its engineering projects.

Hurley remained YouTube's chief executive officer following Google's purchase of the site. However, in fall 2010, he announced he was stepping down from the role but would remain an adviser. While working on YouTube, Hurley also had pursued another project. In 2005, he became a cofounder and chairman of Hlaska, a men's clothing and accessories brand.

YOUTUBE: THE NEW TELEVISION?

In spring 2010, Hurley told a British newspaper "he wanted the site to be watched in the same way as television, up from 15 minutes per day to an average of five hours."[5]

After leaving YouTube, Karim became a student at Stanford University in northern California. There, he completed a master's degree in computer science and continued his studies, working toward a doctoral degree. In 2009, Karim cofounded Youniversity Ventures with Kevin Hartz and Keith Rabois. The company focuses on helping young, innovative, and sometimes student entrepreneurs develop their products through mentoring, networking, and providing capital.

Steve Chen, Chad Hurley, and Jawed Karim now work on projects other than YouTube, but their creation continues to touch the lives of countless people worldwide. In 2007, Hurley told BBC News, "We want to entertain, inform and empower the world through video."[4] From its inception, YouTube has done just that. As YouTube's founders move on to other ventures and explore new possibilities, one can only imagine what the future holds for them. One thing seems certain. The world will likely learn about their new creations online, at the site they created: YouTube. +

In 2008, Hurley and Chen won Vanguard Awards for achievements in new media and technology.

TIMELINE

1977	1978	1979
Chad Hurley is born in Birdsboro, Pennsylvania.	Steven Chen is born in Taipei, Taiwan.	Jawed Karim is born in Merseberg, East Germany (present-day Germany).

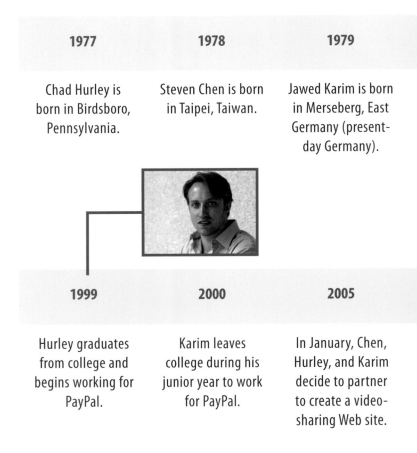

1999	2000	2005
Hurley graduates from college and begins working for PayPal.	Karim leaves college during his junior year to work for PayPal.	In January, Chen, Hurley, and Karim decide to partner to create a video-sharing Web site.

1986

The Chen family moves to the United States and settles in Illinois.

1992

The Karim family moves to the United States and settles in Minnesota.

1998

Chen leaves college before graduating to begin working for PayPal.

2005

Chen, Hurley, and Karim register YouTube LLC and YouTube.com on February 15.

2005

A beta version of the site goes online in spring.

2005

YouTube's first video, "Me at the zoo," is posted on the Web site on April 23.

TIMELINE

2005	2005	2005
In June, four new features are added to YouTube that increase its community quality and appeal to users.	In November, Sequoia Capital provides $3.5 million in funding for YouTube.	YouTube.com officially launches in December.

2006	2006	2008
YouTube has more than 30 million unique visitors in July.	In October, Google buys YouTube for $1.65 billion in stock.	Chen steps down from his position as YouTube's chief technology officer.

2005

Hurley cofounds Hlaska, a men's fashion line.

2006

Sequoia Capital provides $8 million in additional funding in April.

2006

YouTube's headquarters moves out of Hurley's garage to office space in San Mateo, California. The company hires its first employees.

2009

Karim cofounds Youniversity Ventures to encourage young Internet entrepreneurs.

2009

Chen continues to work on projects for Google.

2010

Hurley steps down from his position as YouTube's chief executive officer.

ESSENTIAL FACTS

CREATORS

Chad Meredith Hurley, 1977

Steven Shih Chen, 1978

Jawed Karim, 1979

DATE LAUNCHED

YouTube officially launched its Web site in December 2005.

CHALLENGES

From its beginning, YouTube has faced issues with copyright infringement and appropriateness of content. Deals have been made with some media companies to avoid lawsuits. YouTube has worked to limit piracy with the addition of Audio ID and Video ID. Inappropriate content remains an issue as school districts block access to the site in schools to cut down on cyberbullying. Some governments prevent access to YouTube throughout entire nations to limit access to some information and to protest content deemed offensive for moral or religious reasons.

SUCCESSES

Chen, Hurley, and Karim met as coworkers at PayPal, an Internet start-up company in California. Within a few years of meeting, the three young men were working together at their own company. The entrepreneurs created YouTube, a video-sharing Web site that has changed how computer users worldwide share videos. The site became so popular, it attracted the attention of Internet search company Google, who eventually purchased YouTube for $1.65 billion in stock.

IMPACT ON SOCIETY

YouTube is easy enough for any computer user to navigate. The site has allowed users to connect with friends, family, and strangers worldwide. Some YouTubers have found success, earning recording contracts, for example.

QUOTES

"Our goal is to have YouTube on every screen—to take it from the PC to the living room and the mobile phone."

—*Steve Chen*

"We want to entertain, inform and empower the world through video."

—*Chad Hurley*

"It's very simple: I basically create things that I need myself. It just so happens that sometimes other people want to use that."

—*Jawed Karim*

GLOSSARY

bandwidth

The amount and speed of data transfer.

beta

The last stage of something, such as a Web site, where the software is tested before its final release.

blog

Short for weblog; an online journal or diary.

capital

Money and goods used to finance a business and get or keep it operating.

copyright

The legal right to exclusive ownership of original material, such as art or music; this right controls if and how the material is shared.

dot-com

An Internet-based business; the term comes from the .com that often ends the company's Web address.

hacker

A skilled computer programmer; may also describe a person who illegally breaks into computer systems.

hit

The retrieval of any item from a Web site's server, including a single page or graphic.

launch

> To create a Web site and make it accessible to others.

page view

> A single Web page that has been visited by a single visitor.

personal digital assistant

> A handheld electronic device that helps the user keep personal information, such as appointments, organized.

social networking site

> A Web site where users create profiles and share information with the goal of connecting with other users.

start-up

> A new business.

storage space

> The capacity of hardware to hold data.

URL

> Universal resource locator; the address of a site on the Web.

vlogger

> A person who keeps a video blog.

World Wide Web

> A part of the Internet that uses the rules of hypertext transfer protocol (HTTP) and the computer language hypertext markup language (HTML) to create, display, and link to information. The Web consists of a collection of interconnected sites, pages, and files.

ADDITIONAL RESOURCES

SELECTED BIBLIOGRAPHY

Cloud, John. "The Gurus of YouTube." *Time*. Time Inc., 16 Dec. 2006. Web.

Lashinsky, Adam. "Turning viral videos into a net brand." *CNNMoney.com*. Cable News Network, 11 May 2006. Web.

Miller, Michael. *YouTube 4 You*. Indianapolis, IN: Que, 2007. Print.

FURTHER READINGS

Associated Press. "Google buys YouTube for $1.65 billion." *MSNBC.com*. MSNBC.com, 10 Oct. 2006. Web.

Reinan, John. "Oct. 13, 2006: Whiz Kid: Jawed Karim, a graduate of St. Paul Central." *Startribune.com*. Star Tribune, 8 Feb. 2007. Web.

WEB LINKS

To learn more about YouTube, visit ABDO Publishing Company online at **www.abdopublishing.com.** Web sites about YouTube are featured on our Book Links page. These links are routinely monitored and updated to provide the most current information available.

PLACES TO VISIT

Google
1600 Amphitheatre Parkway, Mountain View, CA 94043
650-253-0000
www.google.com
The company that owns YouTube created the world's most popular Internet search engine.

YouTube
901 Cherry Avenue, San Bruno, CA 94066
650-253-0000
www.youtube.com
This Web site has become a worldwide phenomenon.

SOURCE NOTES

CHAPTER 1. THE WEDDING VIEWED WORLDWIDE

1. Jason DeRusha. "Good Question: How Does A Video Go Viral?" *WCCO*. CBS Broadcasting Inc., 27 Jul. 2009. Web. 22 Aug. 2010.
2. Ibid.
3. Ibid.
4. Adam Hartley. "YouTube is five years old this week." *TechRadar. com*. Future Publishing Limited, 17 May 2010. Web. 8 July 2010.

CHAPTER 2. STEVEN CHEN

1. committee100. "Saturday's Panel: Personal Journey with Steve Chen (2/6)." Video. *YouTube*. YouTube, 18 May 2007. Web. 5 July 2010.
2. John Cloud. "The Gurus of YouTube." *Time*. Time Inc., 16 Dec. 2006. Web. 6 June 2010.
3. Ibid.

CHAPTER 3. CHAD HURLEY

1. Mike Urban. "Reading man makes millions on YouTube." *San Bruno B.A.R.T.* Associated Press, 20 Nov. 2006. Web. 6 Oct. 2010.
2. John Cloud. "The Gurus of YouTube." *Time*. Time Inc., 16 Dec. 2006. Web. 6 June 2010.
3. "Breaking New Ground." *IUP Magazine*. Indiana University of Pennsylvania, Winter 2009. Web. 7 July 2010.
4. Ibid.

CHAPTER 4. JAWED KARIM

1. John Reinan. "Oct. 13, 2006: Whiz Kid: Jawed Karim, a graduate of St. Paul Central." *Startribune.com*. Star Tribune, 8 Feb. 2007. Web. 6 June 2010.
2. Ibid.
3. Miguel Helft. "With YouTube, Student Hits Jackpot Again." *The New York Times*. The New York Times Company, 12 Oct. 2006. Web. 6 June 2010.

CHAPTER 5. MEETING AT PAYPAL

None.

CHAPTER 6. "BROADCAST YOURSELF"

1. David Greising. "YouTube founder rides video clips to dot-com riches." *Chicago Tribune*. Chicago Tribune, 15 Oct. 2006. Web. 6 June 2010.

2. jawed. "Me at the zoo." Video. *YouTube*. YouTube, 23 Apr. 2005. Web. 6 June 2010.

CHAPTER 7. SOCIAL IMPACT

1. Miguel Helft. "With YouTube, Student Hits Jackpot Again." *The New York Times*. The New York Times Company, 12 Oct. 2006. Web. 6 June 2010.

2. John Cloud. "The Gurus of YouTube." *Time*. Time Inc., 16 Dec. 2006. Web. 6 June 2010.

3. "Joining the YouTube Community—And Creating Your Own Channel." Book Excerpt. *InformIT*. Pearson Education, Informit, 16 Apr. 2007. Web. 6 Oct. 2010.

4. Darren Waters. "Video service YouTube grows up." *BBC*. BBC, 20 June 2007. Web. 6 June 2010.

5. Carly Mayberry. "Daly Expands Domain With Net Projects." *AllBusiness*. AllBusiness.com, 27 Nov. 2006. Web. 6 June 2010.

6. Darren Waters. "Video service YouTube grows up." *BBC*. BBC, 20 June 2007. Web. 6 June 2010.

CHAPTER 8. SOLD!

1. Adam Lashinsky. "Turning viral videos into a net brand." *CNNMoney.com*. Cable News Network, 11 May 2006. Web. 20 June 2010.

2. Belinda Goldsmith. "YouTube presents awards to its first stars." *Reuters*. Thomson Reuters, 26 Mar. 2007. Web. 21 June 2010.

3. Anne Broache. "SNL cult hit yanked from video-sharing site." *Cnet.com*. CBS Interactive, 17 Feb. 2006. Web. 23 May 2010.

SOURCE NOTES CONTINUED

4. Lev Grossman. "Time's Person of the Year: You." *Time*. Time Inc., 13 Dec. 2006. Web. 17 June 2010.

5. Jim Hopkins. "Surprise! There's a third YouTube co-founder." *USAToday*. USA TODAY, 11 Oct. 2006. Web. 17 June 2010.

6. "google." *Merriam-Webster*. Merriam-Webster, Incorporated, 2010. Web. 21 June 2010.

7. Associated Press. "Google buys YouTube for $1.65 billion." *MSNBC.com*. MSNBC.com, 10 Oct. 2006. Web. 11 Oct. 2010.

8. John Cloud. "The Gurus of YouTube." *Time*. Time Inc., 16 Dec. 2006. Web. 6 June 2010.

9. Associated Press. "Google buys YouTube for $1.65 billion." *MSNBC.com*. MSNBC.com, 10 Oct. 2006. Web. 11 Oct. 2010.

CHAPTER 9. NEW OWNER, SAME YOUTUBE

1. Brian Stelter. "YouTube Videos Pull in Real Money." *The New York Times*. The New York Times Company, 10 Dec. 2008. Web. 22 Aug. 2010.

2. "YouTube Elevates Most Popular Users to Partners." Blog. *YouTube*. YouTube Inc., 3 May 2007. Web. 20 June 2010.

3. Emma Barnett. "Top 10 facts you didn't know about YouTube." *Telegraph.co.uk*. Telegraph Media Group Limited, 17 May 2010. Web. 23 May 2010.

4. Catherine Rampell. "YouTubers Try a Different Forum: Real Life." *The Washington Post*. The Washington Post Company, 10 Sept. 2007. Web. 13 June 2010.

5. "Safety Center." *YouTube*. YouTube, LLC, 2010. Web. 20 June 2010.

6. Andrew Colley. "States still hold out on YouTube." *AustralianIT*. News Limited, 6 March 2007. Web. 20 June 2010.

7. Darren Waters. "Video service YouTube grows up." *BBC*. BBC, 20 June 2007. Web. 8 June 2010.

CHAPTER 10. POLITICS, POP MUSIC, AND BEYOND

1. Mike Sachoff. "YouTube's Role in Election 2008." *WebProNews*. iEntry Network, 1 Mar. 2007. Web. 8 July 2010.

2. Ibid.

3. Emma Barnett. "Top 10 facts you didn't know about YouTube." *Telegraph.co.uk*. Telegraph Media Group Limited, 17 May 2010. Web. 23 May 2010.

4. Mike Sachoff. "YouTube's Role in Election 2008." *WebProNews*. iEntry Network, 1 Mar. 2007. Web. 8 July 2010.

5. Adam Toren. "Profile on Chad Hurley." *Youngentrepreneur*. Youngentrepreneur.com Inc., 17 Nov. 2009. Web. 20 June 2010.

INDEX

Andreessen, Marc, 22, 36, 37
AOL, 63–64
"Ask a Ninja" video, 69

Bieber, Justin, 83
  "Baby" video, 83
Brodack, Brooke, 62–63, 83
  "Crazed Numa Fan!!!!" video,
    62–63
Brolsma, Gary, 62
  "Numa Numa Dance" video, 62
Buckley, Michael, 80

Chen, Steven, 8, 13, 16–22, 26,
    30, 38, 40, 41, 44, 46–54, 57,
    58, 63, 68, 70–72, 74–75, 78,
    86, 93, 94
  childhood, 16–18
  education, 19–21
computer animation, 25, 27, 28
Confinity, 21–22, 28, 38, 41
  Levchin, Max, 21–22, 44, 49
  PayPal, 21–22, 28, 38, 41–44,
    46, 49, 54
Craigslist, 53

Daly, Carson, 63
Denters, Esmee, 83
Digital Millennium Copyright Act,
    91

eBay, 42–43
  Omidyar, Pierre, 43
  purchase of PayPal, 42–43

Facebook, 10, 14, 54, 56–57

going viral, 9, 10, 11, 14, 75, 91
Google, 58, 63–64, 71, 73–75, 78,
    81, 90, 91, 93
  purchase of YouTube, 71–75, 78,
    81, 93
  stock, 72, 75
  verb, 73

"Here It Goes Again" video, 69
home computer use, 13–14, 41
Hurley, Chad, 8, 13, 24–30, 38,
    40–41, 43–44, 46–54, 57–58,
    68, 70–72, 74, 75, 78, 89, 92,
    93–94
  childhood, 24–26
  education, 26–27

Illinois Mathematics and Science
    Academy, 19–22

"JK Wedding Entrance Dance"
    video, 6–14
  Heinz, Kevin, 6–12, 82–83
  Peterson, Jill, 6–12, 82–83
  views, 8–10

Karim, Jawed, 8, 13, 30, 32–38,
    40–44, 46, 48–54, 57–58, 73,
    75, 93–94
  childhood, 32–35
  education, 35–37
  parents, 32–34, 37

"Kiwi" video, 69
Kovalchick Convention and
    Athletic Complex, 30
Kutcher, Ashton, 10

Lady Gaga, 11
"Lazy Sunday: The Chronicles of
    Narnia" video, 69–70
LiveJournal, 56

memes, 14
MSN, 63–64
MySpace, 53, 56–57, 72

NBC, 10, 70
Netscape, 36
Nyberg, Jake, 9, 12

Palm Pilot, 41, 42
personal digital assistant, 41–42

Sequoia Capital, 49, 54, 57
"Smosh" video, 69

"Terranaomi" video, 69
Thank You for Smoking, 44
Twitter, 10, 14

"Unexpected Divorce Intro" video,
    14
University of Illinois at Urbana-
    Champaign, 20–22, 36–37, 44

Web advertising, 74–75
Web design, 25, 27, 28
Wikipedia, 72
Williams, Cory, 80

Xanga, 56

Yahoo!, 49, 63–64
Youniversity Ventures, 94
YouTube
    blocked access, 84–86
    celebrities, 61–63, 83
    channels, 59, 86, 89
    concept, 47–49
    content appropriateness, 67–68,
        84–86, 93
    copyright issues, 13, 68–70, 72,
        91
    copyright policies, 81, 93
    criticism, 67–68, 91, 93
    development, 48–49, 53–54
    FiveYear Channel, 90–91
    gatherings, 83–84
    launch, 49–52
    media company deals, 72, 79
    motto, 51–52
    role in politics, 59, 89–90
    sale to Google, 71–75, 78, 81,
        93
YouTubers, 79–80, 83

ABOUT THE AUTHOR

Rebecca Rowell has a Master of Arts in Publishing and Writing from Emerson College. She has edited numerous nonfiction children's books, including several biographies. Born and raised in Minneapolis, Minnesota, she has lived in Arizona, Massachusetts, and Austria. She once again lives in Minneapolis.

PHOTO CREDITS